The Library of
ASTRONAUT BIOGRAPHIES™

ELLEN OCHOA

The First Hispanic Woman in Space

Joy Paige

rosen
central™

The Rosen Publishing Group, Inc., New York

To Scott—a first-rate boyfriend and
best friend. You're absolutely tops.

Published in 2004 by The Rosen Publishing Group, Inc.
29 East 21st Street, New York, NY 10010

First Edition

Library of Congress Cataloging-in-Publication Data

Paige, Joy.
Ellen Ochoa: the first Hispanic woman in space / Joy Paige. — 1st ed.
   v. cm. — (The library of astronaut biographies) Includes
bibliographical references and index. Contents: A dream of success—
Getting a good education—Laying the groundwork—Joining
NASA—Up in space—Conclusion: A new beginning.
ISBN 0-8239-4457-3 (library binding)
1. Ochoa, Ellen—Juvenile literature. 2. Women astronauts—United
States—Biography—Juvenile literature. 3. Astronauts—United
States—Biography—Juvenile literature. 4. Hispanic American
women—Biography—Juvenile literature. [1. Ochoa, Ellen. 2.
Women—Biography. 3. Astronauts. 4. Hispanic Americans—Biog-
raphy.] I. Title. II. Series.
TL789.85.O25P34 2004
629.45'0092—dc21

2003010700

Manufactured in the United States of America

CONTENTS

A DREAM OF SUCCESS

In 1968, when Ellen Ochoa was ten years old, the United States sent three astronauts to orbit the Moon for the first time in history. The mission was called *Apollo 8*. It was designed to explore and photograph the Moon's surface in advance of a lunar landing—a feat that had not yet been accomplished—during the later *Apollo 11* mission. If public interest in *Apollo 8* was high, it was surpassed one year later when Neil Armstrong and Buzz Aldrin became the first men

This is a photograph of the lunar surface taken from the *Apollo 8* spacecraft in 1968. This was the first time in history that humans orbited the Moon, an achievement that inspired a young Ellen Ochoa to reach for the stars.

in history to walk on the Moon during *Apollo 11*. All of America was tuned in to learn what the astronauts would discover up there and if they would return safely. Ellen Ochoa was one of those Americans riveted to the radio and television.

Although Ellen Ochoa would one day become an astronaut, she did not decide at an early age that this was her calling in life. After all, when she was growing up, there were no female astronauts—the field was dominated exclusively by men. In addition, Ochoa was Hispanic, and no minorities had participated in the early days of the American space program. To top it all off, thousands of people wanted to be astronauts, but only a select few would actually pass the physical, technical, and psychological tests necessary to be accepted into the space program and then complete the years-long mission training.

Space exploration was a very competitive field. During the days when Ochoa was seriously focused on a career as an astronaut, there were many hurdles for her to jump. But as a young girl, Ellen Ochoa was not focused on getting accepted into the National Aeronautics and Space Administration

(NASA; the government agency devoted to space exploration and manned space flights). Instead, she concentrated simply on getting a good education and contributing to humanity in some way. In pursuing these goals, however, Ochoa was drawn irresistibly into the American space program.

Ellen Ochoa spent her youth excelling in school and passionately pursuing her hobbies. She was known for her dedication to her studies and the excellent grades she earned as a result of her hard work. She was also known as a talented musician and athlete. Her curiosity and constant desire to learn took her to college at San Diego State University and then to graduate school at Stanford University in northern California. It was at Stanford where she first heard that NASA was accepting applications to the space program. After successfully completing the strenuous application process, Ochoa was accepted by NASA and made history by becoming the first Hispanic female astronaut.

Not only did Ellen Ochoa become the first Hispanic female astronaut, along the way she also became a scientist, a doctor, an inventor, an engineer, and a physicist, not to mention a mother and a wife. Ochoa credits her own mother, Roseanne, with giving her the desire to learn and the belief that she could achieve the highest goals she set for herself. Roseanne told her five children that getting an education would provide them with great opportunities. She taught this lesson by example; while raising a family, Roseanne spent many years

The United States's attempt to put a man on the Moon captivated the public imagination and riveted its attention. In this picture a young boy wearing a toy space helmet watches a broadcast of the first televised pictures of the Moon's surface in history. The pictures were provided by an unmanned NASA probe, the *Ranger 9*, in 1965.

taking college classes part-time, eventually earning three college degrees.

After becoming an astronaut, Ellen Ochoa spent a lot of time talking to schoolchildren, sharing with them the wisdom that her mother had offered her. She encouraged kids to get a good education and set high goals for themselves so that they could develop interests and skills and succeed in their chosen field just as she had done. According to *Contemporary Heroes and Heroines, Book IV*, Ochoa said, "I do as much speaking as I am allowed to do. I tell students that the opportunities I had were a result of having a good educational background. Education is what allows you to stand out." These days, Ochoa travels a lot, encouraging kids to learn as much as possible and not to give up on their dreams.

The story of Ellen's Ochoa's rise to greatness is an inspiring tale. From humble beginnings, Ochoa's perseverance, intelligence, curiosity, and strength helped her to climb to the top of her field. From that lofty height, she was able to reach the stars.

CHAPTER 1

GETTING A GOOD EDUCATION

Ellen Ochoa was born on May 10, 1958, in Los Angeles, California. Though she was born in Los Angeles, she grew up in La Mesa, near San Diego. Ellen was one of five children in the Ochoa household.

Ellen's mother was born in Oklahoma. Her father was born in the United States but was of Mexican heritage. Though Ellen was Hispanic, she never learned to speak Spanish. She spoke of her father and her ethnic heritage in an interview with Scholastic.com:

My Hispanic roots come from my father's side. His parents were Mexican, but my father was born in this country. He was one of twelve children. My father grew up speaking both Spanish and English, but, unfortunately, he didn't speak Spanish with us at home. When I was growing up, my father believed as many people did at the time that there was a prejudice against people speaking their native language. It's really too bad, and I'm glad that things have changed in recent years.

While her father was concerned about ethnic prejudice, Ochoa does not believe her heritage either helped or prevented her from achieving her goals. In a December 1, 1993, article by Lydia Martin for the the Knight-Ridder/Tribune News Service, Ochoa said: "Getting to be an astronaut is tough for anybody, not just Hispanics or women. I don't think my background made it harder or easier. I think it's just a matter of working hard to have a very good education." Many people might think that being a member of a minority group could have held Ochoa back from breaking into NASA, but she refuses to accept that line of thinking. She believes in herself enough to know that she can do anything she puts her mind to.

By all accounts, it was Roseanne Ochoa who instilled this self-confidence and drive to succeed in Ellen. Roseanne made sure each of her kids got a good education. The Ochoa children were taught to reach for their goals, and this wisdom was not wasted on Ellen. In a 1990 article in the *San Diego Union-Tribune*, Ellen said, "My mom's been a big influence on me in that she had to raise five kids a lot of the time on her own. And she stressed that education is important and that it opens up a lot of options." Ellen names her mother as her biggest role model. After all, Roseanne taught Ellen that there was no room for self-doubt when aspiring to greatness. Her mother did nothing less than encourage Ellen to reach for the stars.

At an early age, Ellen learned the importance of working hard. While raising her family mostly by herself, Roseanne Ochoa took college classes for twenty-three years, eventually earning three degrees from San Diego State University. Though Roseanne had many responsibilities, she always made time to learn. During Ellen's preflight interview with NASA before her fourth shuttle mission, she said,

I had a number of teachers that certainly encouraged me in specific areas, or just overall were important influences, but I think the number one influence would be my mother, partly just because of the way she raised me and my four siblings and partly because of her love of learning. She went to college part-time for twenty years, and finally graduated a couple of years after I did. And it was just because she was interested in all the courses that the school had to offer and wanted to learn more.

Obviously, Roseanne Ochoa's desire to learn and absorb information rubbed off on her daughter. Throughout her life, Ellen has always strived to continue to learn new things.

Early School Experiences

One of Ellen Ochoa's favorite books as a child was *A Wrinkle in Time*, by Madeleine L'Engle. This famous book is about three children who travel through space and time to rescue the father of two of the children. The space travel element of the story intrigued Ellen as a young girl and struck a chord

HISPANIC SPACE PIONEER

Although Ellen Ochoa was the first Hispanic woman to leave Earth's atmosphere, she was not the first Hispanic person to reach space. That honor goes to Franklin Chang-Díaz, who, in 1986, was a crew member on the space shuttle *Columbia*.

Chang-Díaz was born in Costa Rica on April 5, 1950. Like Ochoa, he concentrated on getting a good education. He graduated from Colegio De La Salle in San José, Costa Rica, in 1967, and from Hartford High School in Hartford, Connecticut, in 1969. In 1973, Chang-Díaz earned his bachelor of science degree in mechanical engineering from the University of Connecticut. Years later, in 1977, he received a doctorate in applied plasma physics from the Massachusetts Institute of Technology.

In May 1980, Chang-Díaz was selected to become a part of the NASA space program. He trained for a year before becoming an astronaut, though he did not get to go up into space until the

Columbia STS 61-C mission in 1986. Since that first space flight, Chang-Díaz has taken part in six other space missions. His most recent trip to space, in 2002, was aboard the space shuttle *Endeavor*. On this mission he performed three space walks—totaling nineteen hours outside the shuttle—to install equipment on the International Space Station (a large orbiting scientific research center, supported, built, and staffed by sixteen nations).

Being an astronaut, in turn, made him want to develop closer ties between the astronaut community and the science community. As a result, he helped form the Astronaut Science Support Group, for which he was the director until January 1989.

In addition to being the first Hispanic astronaut, Chang-Díaz has also participated in more space missions than anyone else in the world. He has logged over 1,600 hours in space!

with her. In fact, *A Wrinkle in Time* may very well have been one of the inspirations for her desire to become an astronaut.

While in junior high school, Ellen's parents divorced, and she went to live with her mother. Though this must have been a tough transition for the adolescent girl, her schoolwork never suffered. Ellen remained an excellent student, always hungry to learn. Her favorite subjects included music and math. In her spare time, she enjoyed reading and playing the flute. When Ellen was thirteen years old, she won the San Diego spelling bee. She also was granted the distinction of Outstanding Seventh and Eighth Grade Student by her junior high school. By all accounts, she was an outstanding student, always working hard and getting good grades.

Ellen attended Grossmont High School in La Mesa, California, where she quickly became known for being the best math student in her school. Ellen enjoyed studying math, although she noted in an interview with *La Prensa San Diego*, "Usually, girls weren't encouraged to go to college and major in math and science. My high school calculus teacher, Ms. Paz Jensen, made math appealing and motivated me to continue studying it in college." Ochoa credits her high school teachers with helping her learn by making learning fun and exciting. "I was always drawn to teachers who made class interesting," she said. "In high school, I enjoyed my American and English literature classes because my teachers, Jeanne Dorsey and Dani Barton, created an environment where interaction was important."

Even with her dedication to schoolwork, she did manage to make time for extracurricular activities. During her high school years, she was asked to play flute with the Civic Youth Orchestra in San Diego. Ellen played the flute very well and became an accomplished classical flutist.

Ellen graduated from Grossmont High School in 1975. She was the valedictorian of her graduating class. This meant she had the highest grades of all her fellow students. People took notice of Ellen. Her drive and determination must have stood out, as did her excellent grades and numerous honors and awards. One of the most competitive and selective colleges in the United

States—Stanford University—recognized her talent and achievement and actively recruited her. Ochoa's many years of hard work and study were already beginning to pay off.

Excelling in College

Ochoa was offered a four-year scholarship to Stanford University for her undergraduate education. Stanford is an excellent school, and Ochoa must have been both flattered and extremely tempted by the offer, but in the end she turned it down so that she could stay near her home and be close to her family. Ochoa wanted to help her mother care for her younger siblings. After all, she had received so much help and encouragement from her mother throughout her youth. Now Ochoa wanted to pass along to her brothers and sisters the ideals her mother had instilled in her. It was important to Ochoa that each of her siblings received a good education. Her presence and encouragement must have helped, for she was not to remain the only scholar of the Ochoa household. Each of the Ochoas now has a college degree.

This is a view of the clock tower on the campus of San Diego State University in California. Ellen Ochoa turned down an offer from prestigious Stanford University in favor of San Diego State so that she could remain close to her family while pursuing her undergraduate education. She would graduate in 1980 at the very top of her class.

Ochoa's interest in math, science, and family brought her to San Diego State University. At first, Ochoa considered studying engineering—the application of scientific and mathematical principles to practical things, such as machines. She was soon steered away from the field, however, when one of her professors told her it was a bad choice for a woman because it was too "complicated."

19

At San Diego State, Ellen Ochoa switched her major several times, moving from music to business, journalism, English, and computer science before finally settling on physics. In this photograph, Ochoa can be seen conducting an optics experiment with a fellow physics student.

This professor obviously misjudged the highly intelligent and driven young woman standing before him.

Ochoa went on to study physics instead. Physics is the study of the interaction between matter and energy. Though it is a very difficult field of study, Ochoa was not put off by the challenge. "I found my niche then," said Ochoa in a GraduatingEngineer.com article. "In my undergraduate days at SDSU, I explored several majors before choosing physics. But when I took a physics class for non-majors, it grabbed my interest so fast that I wanted to find out how to apply math to a scientific field."

At the same time that Ochoa was studying at San Diego State University, her mother was also studying there. Roseanne Ochoa graduated from San Diego State University in 1982, two years after Ellen graduated with top honors. As in high school, Ellen had achieved the extremely difficult feat of being valedictorian of her graduating class.

After graduating from college, many students feel they have had more than enough schoolwork and take time off to travel or they jump right into their

ASTRONAUT ALUMNI

Mae Jemison and Sally Ride, two of Ellen Ochoa's fellow female astronauts, also attended Stanford University. Mae Jemison started at Stanford in 1973 when she was only sixteen years old. She went on to earn degrees in both chemical engineering and African American studies in 1977. Jemison was the first African American woman in space.

Sally Ride received four degrees from Stanford University. She received a bachelor of arts in English and a bachelor of science in physics in 1973, a master of science in physics in 1975, and a doctorate in physics in 1978. Ride was the first American woman in space.

Astronaut Steve Smith graduated from Stanford in 1981 with a bachelor of science in electrical engineering. He also earned a master of science in electrical engineering in 1982 and a master's degree in business administration in 1987, also from Stanford. He joined NASA in 1989.

These are just a few of the Stanford students that ended up at NASA. As of 2003, eighteen NASA astronauts have attended Stanford University.

careers. However, in keeping with her mother's philosophy—that getting a good education is of the utmost importance—Ochoa continued her studies. This time she would not resist the call of Stanford, which was once again pursuing her, and would not turn the school down. In 1980, Ochoa entered Stanford University's graduate program.

Early Lessons

Being offered a position in Stanford's graduate program was the greatest of Ellen Ochoa's many early triumphs. From an early age, Ellen Ochoa learned the lessons that would inspire and help her throughout her life. Her mother provided her with the knowledge that she could succeed at anything she truly put her mind to. Roseanne Ochoa vividly illustrated this point to Ellen by providing a great example of how hard work can help a person accomplish whatever he or she sets out to do.

Ellen's intelligence and desire to learn were apparent from an early age. She enjoyed learning and absorbed information like a sponge. Her interest in science and math set her apart at an early age, as these were subjects in which only boys were thought to be talented and interested. Even in high school, Ellen was crossing gender boundaries and taking on academic challenges with a dedication and maturity that were beyond her years.

Throughout Ellen's childhood, she learned that in order to succeed, you have to work hard. This knowledge helped her as an astronaut, a scientist, and even as a mother. Ellen Ochoa's drive and dedication are truly inspiring.

CHAPTER 2

LAYING THE GROUNDWORK

Ellen Ochoa began her graduate studies at Stanford University in 1980, immediately after finishing her undergraduate physics studies at San Diego State University. She decided on Stanford because she wished to attend a university that featured a diverse student body and offered a comprehensive range of courses and programs in both the arts and sciences. Because she had an interest in the humanities—such as music—she did not want to attend a technical institute that had a narrow focus. Throughout her life, no matter what course work or professional project she was focusing on,

Ochoa always made time for hobbies and outside interests, especially her music.

Graduate school is a difficult challenge for even the best students. It takes a certain kind of dedication and determination to succeed in graduate school. Graduate students have chosen to be there because they excel in their chosen field and wish to dig even deeper, gaining very specialized knowledge. The work is often self-directed, independent, and solitary, so graduate students must be very disciplined and self-motivated. Ochoa was the perfect candidate for success.

Ochoa was talented in so many subjects that she switched majors many times during her undergraduate career, trying out different areas of study to see how much she liked them before settling on physics. Although she excelled in science and math, she remained curious about other fields. Ochoa allowed herself to explore her options and get a feel for what she liked best. The combination of her curiosity, talent, and determination to succeed made her a very unique individual and a superb graduate student.

Studies at Stanford

Ochoa began her studies at Stanford wanting to try her hand at engineering, which would put her math skills to use. The words of discouragement offered by her San Diego State professor remained with her, but she now regretted letting this professor convince her that engineering would be too hard for a woman to master. This time around, Ochoa would not let anyone talk her out of studying engineering. Though it may sound like a complicated course of study, as her San Diego State professor warned, to Ochoa it was just another challenge. Never in her life would Ellen Ochoa let a challenge get in the way of trying something new and interesting.

One of Ochoa's interests during graduate school was in a mathematical tool called Fourier transforms, an engineering formula that is used in antenna studies, optics, and astronomy, as well as other fields related to physics. Joseph Goodman, Ochoa's graduate advisor and a leading figure in the field of Fourier optics, encouraged her to pursue this line of study. Goodman's influence helped Ochoa become

This is a photograph of White Plaza on the campus of Stanford University in California. Ellen Ochoa earned her master's degree in electrical engineering from Stanford in 1981. She remained at the school to pursue her doctorate in electrical engineering, which she earned in 1985 when she was only twenty-seven years old.

involved in optical computing research, a field in which her work would become very well known.

After earning her master's degree in 1981, Ochoa remained at Stanford to continue studying electrical engineering. She earned her Ph.D. in electrical engineering in 1985. She was officially a doctor, at the age of twenty–seven! Ochoa was still very young and had already earned three higher degrees. She had not taken a single break from school since entering kindergarten, but instead had pursued her demanding and complex studies with tireless determination and energy.

This intensive studying and concentration on difficult subjects was helping Ochoa prepare for her work as an astronaut. Astronauts perform an enormous amount of technical and scientific work in space, often under intense time pressure. Ochoa was gaining the technical knowledge she would need on a space mission and developing the grace under pressure necessary for mission success and survival.

Why do astronauts need to be good at physics, math, or electrical engineering? Astronauts perform a wide variety of difficult jobs while in space. They do not just travel in space shuttles, orbit Earth a few times, enjoy the view, and come back down. While in space, astronauts perform scientific studies that help us gain a better understanding of the natural processes of both Earth and space. These scientific studies help reveal how we are affected by what happens in space. Ochoa's broad knowledge— gained through years of undergraduate and graduate study and a lifetime

of curiosity—would soon serve her well as an astronaut trainee and, later, in space.

Going to Work

In 1985, after earning her Ph.D. from Stanford, Ellen Ochoa went to work at Sandia National Laboratories in Albuquerque, New Mexico, as a research engineer. There, she helped develop an optical system to be used in guiding robots. Basically, she gave robots "sight." The optical system enabled robots to identify and locate objects around them. Ochoa worked with a number of well-known and influential research scientists on this project. In fact, a number of Sandia engineers, including Ochoa, were recognized as some of the top twenty Hispanics working in technology by *Hispanic Engineer & Information Technology* magazine.

For her work with these optical systems, Ochoa and several other engineers received three patents for three separate optical devices. A patent is an official document issued by the government stating that an invention can be used and sold only by the inventor.

Having received her Ph.D. from Stanford University in 1985, Ellen Ochoa soon went to work as a research engineer for Sandia National Laboratories in Albuquerque, New Mexico *(pictured above)*. Sandia is a government-owned and government-operated facility mostly devoted to military technology.

Ochoa is now known for her specialized knowledge in this particular field, which is directly based upon research she did for her doctoral dissertation at Stanford. In fact, one of her patents is shared with her graduate advisor, Joseph Goodman, and one of her professors, Bert Hesselink.

In *The Ellen Ochoa Video Documentary*, Ochoa explained her optical system research:

While I was at Stanford and I was working before becoming an astronaut, I was involved in doing research in equipment like lasers and holograms . . . And we were looking at those specifically for processing images—for example, trying to find a particular object within an image. You might use that on a manufacturing line if you're trying to inspect equipment and you're looking for defects, or you might use it on an autonomous lander to Mars when you're trying to land around a particular spot and you're using a video camera to look for it. And you can use optics to help you find the right place. Those were the kinds of things I was looking for and those were what some of my patents are in.

Application to NASA

Ochoa's working life was turning out to be as challenging, exciting, and successful as her education had been. As always, the process of continuing to learn was fulfilling for her. Curiosity and intellectual restlessness are also constants in Ochoa's life. Though she was making great strides in her research, she also began to dream of becoming an astronaut.

SANDIA NATIONAL LABORATORIES

Sandia National Laboratories is a government-owned and government-operated facility with two locations: one in Albuquerque, New Mexico, and one in Livermore, California. Ellen Ochoa worked at the Albuquerque location during her time with Sandia, from 1985 to 1988.

Sandia, then called Z Division, was created in 1945 at the time of the Manhattan Project, the United States's atom bomb development project. Sandia employees worked to ensure that the nation's weapons stockpile was safe and secure. They also did research to help improve the weapons that were available. Throughout the years, the engineers and scientists at Sandia National Laboratories developed many new technologies that improved weapons safety and accuracy.

While Ochoa was a graduate student at Stanford, she had learned from friends that NASA was accepting applications for its space program. She had never before considered becoming an astronaut, but she suddenly became very interested in applying. Ochoa found out that NASA was looking for people who, like her, were extremely skilled and experienced in math and science. She sought out more information about how NASA chooses its astronauts and decided to apply right after she received her Ph.D. in electrical engineering in 1985.

Ochoa was not accepted the first time she applied, but she decided to keep trying. In the meantime, she continued her flute playing and even learned to fly an airplane. Obtaining her private pilot's license could only help her chances of being accepted by NASA. More than at any time before in her life, Ochoa's diversity of interests would begin to pay off. She was not aware of it at the time, but her many outside interests, such as music and sports, would help her get into NASA's program. Aside from its strict academic requirements, NASA also looks for well-rounded individuals, people who are good at many different things, both physical tasks and mental challenges. The ideal NASA candidate is comfortable working in many different disciplines—often simultaneously—in a range of environments. An astronaut may have to compute his or her own calculations if a computer fails during a spaceflight, or may have to leave the capsule on a space walk to fix a damaged piece of equipment on the spacecraft. Ellen Ochoa—fearless, focused, and smart—would fit the bill perfectly. She just had to convince NASA of that fact.

DISASTER!

Soon after Ellen Ochoa submitted her first application to NASA, tragedy struck the space program in January 1986. The space shuttle *Challenger* had been sent into space nine times before it was chosen for mission 51-L. This mission was very similar to other missions, with the usual long list of experiments and tasks. For the first time in NASA history, however, a civilian would be on board with the astronauts. Sharon Christa McAuliffe was chosen to join the shuttle program as part of the Teacher in Space Program

The space shuttle *Challenger* explodes seventy-three seconds after launch from the Kennedy Space Center on January 28, 1986. All seven crew members, including Christa McAuliffe, the first school teacher selected to go into space, died in the explosion.

(TISP). She was to be the first teacher to soar into space.

The *Challenger* carried mission commander Francis R. Scobee; pilot Michael J. Smith; mission specialists Ronald E. McNair, Ellison S. Onizuka, and Judith A. Resnik; and payload specialist Gregory B. Jarvis. McAuliffe was also a mission specialist. These seven astronauts were due to take off on January 22, 1986, but were postponed numerous times due to various equipment problems and bad weather. Finally, on January 28, 1986, the space shuttle *Challenger* took off into a crystal clear blue sky. To the shock and horror of the hundreds of people witnessing the launch at Cape Kennedy and the millions more watching on television, the shuttle exploded only seventy-three seconds into its flight. Everyone on board the spacecraft died instantly. Investigators eventually concluded that a faulty O-ring seal on the shuttle's booster rocket contributed to the explosion.

News about the disaster traveled quickly around the country, especially in America's schools where many classes had tuned in to watch the first teacher travel to space. U.S. president Ronald Reagan quickly addressed the nation to express his sadness over the tragedy. In a televised speech he said, "Today is a day for mourning and remembering. Nancy [Reagan's wife] and I are pained to the core over the tragedy of the shuttle *Challenger*. We know we share this pain with all of the people of our country. This is truly a national loss."

A SECOND SHUTTLE DISASTER

Unfortunately, the *Challenger* disaster was not the only fatal accident in the space shuttle program. On February 1, 2003, the space shuttle *Columbia*, the oldest active shuttle in the fleet, disintegrated as it was reentering Earth's atmosphere. The entire mission had gone almost flawlessly, but something went terribly wrong as the space shuttle passed high above the Pacific Ocean on its way to a landing in Florida. The leading edge of the shuttle's left wing may have been damaged during takeoff by a chunk of foam insulation that had fallen off the shuttle's fuel tank and struck the spacecraft. The intensely heated gasses associated with reentry may have entered the shuttle through the damaged portion of the wing, leading to a massive heating and breakup of the vehicle. The seven astronauts, including the first Israeli astronaut in history, were all killed.

PRESSING ON

Ellen Ochoa was undaunted after the *Challenger* disaster and continued to pursue her dream of becoming an astronaut. She was well aware of the dangers of space flight when she took her first trip to space in 1993 and during her three subsequent shuttle missions. In characteristic style, she trusts in her training, courage, and sense of adventure to get her through any emergency. As she told Scholastic.com,

This is a plaque dedicated to the memory of the seven shuttle astronauts killled in the 1986 *Challenger* explosion.

There's never really been anything for me to be scared of because nothing has ever gone wrong on any of my missions. For me, going into space is very exciting, not scary. The riskiest part of the flight is the launch because it's the phase of the flight when things are most likely to go wrong. But like I said,

there have never been problems on my missions, and besides, we are trained to handle any problems that might come along.

Perseverance Pays Off

Beginning in 1985, Ellen Ochoa sent in an application to NASA every year. The application process had been rigorous. To apply for the program, one must complete and mail in many different forms. After the applications are received and evaluated, some of the applicants are called in for weeklong interviews and medical examinations. Astronauts must be in perfect health to be able to go into space. The atmosphere in space is much different than the atmosphere here on Earth, and it places unfamiliar stresses on the human body.

While waiting for an invitation into NASA's astronaut program, Ochoa went to work for one of NASA's research laboratories, the Ames Research Center. As a research engineer, she led a team of thirty-five engineers and scientists. Her background in physics and electrical engineering made her a valued member of the team at Ames, where she helped develop computer systems designed for aeronautical expeditions. She eventually rose to the position of chief of the information sciences division. By 1989, Ochoa had been given the honor of the Hispanic Engineer National Achievement Award for Most Promising Engineer in Government. Her hard work was definitely paying off, and the NASA astronaut program could not deny her for much longer.

It was not until 1990—five years after she sent in her first application—that Ochoa was chosen as one of the top 100 candidates out of a pool of 2,000 applicants. These 100 hopeful men and women would be examined further and weeded out. Only 23 people made the final cut. Ochoa was one of them.

CHAPTER 3

JOINING NASA

Ellen Ochoa was chosen to be part of NASA's space program in 1990 and officially became an astronaut in 1991. By this time, NASA had become more open to accepting women into the program. Sally Ride was the first female American astronaut. She was launched into space on the space shuttle *Challenger* mission in 1983. Ride was one of Ochoa's heroes. Ochoa would follow in her footsteps by being chosen for the *Discovery* mission in 1993, ten years after Ride's historic space flight. Usually, new astronauts have to train for ten or more years before being sent on their first mission, but Ochoa got lucky and was scheduled to be part of a mission only three years after becoming an astronaut.

By this time, Ochoa was only thirty-three years old and had already accomplished so much in such a short time. She had a master's degree and a Ph.D. from a prestigious university, she held three patents for optical systems she helped develop, and she had been accepted

Sally Ride communicates with ground control during her history-making flight aboard the space shuttle *Challenger* in 1983. She had become the first American woman to travel into space.

ted into NASA's space program. Now she would embark on a whole new path in her life and use all the knowledge she had gained to explore space. Ellen Ochoa was in for a very exciting adventure.

Ellen Ochoa, Astronaut

Ellen Ochoa officially became an astronaut in July 1991, a year and a half after being selected by NASA for the space program. Before taking part in a mission, Ochoa would have to undergo an intense training period. Astronaut training is extremely difficult and challenging because it prepares astronauts for anything and everything that may happen in space, the expected and the unexpected. Crew members' lives are at stake when traveling in space, and astronauts need to be prepared for the worst.

Space shuttle trainees are taught the ins and outs of the many complex mechanical, electrical, hydraulic, and electronic systems on the spacecraft. They must learn how to recognize when something has gone wrong and how to fix any problems that may occur. It is mentally exhausting to learn so much technical information so quickly. Training is also physically demanding, as trainees are given a glimpse into what it will be like to live in weightlessness for an extended period of time. With the help of simulators, they can also experience the sheer, violent force of both takeoff and reentry.

Ochoa described the rigors of space training in a 1999 interview with Scholastic.com: "Everything is always harder to do in training. In training, we

On July 16, 1990, the first day of astronaut candidate training at the Johnson Space Center in Houston, Texas, Ellen Ochoa stands with fellow candidate Eileen Collins. Ochoa would go on to become the first Hispanic woman astronaut, while Collins would become NASA's first female pilot candidate.

prepare for anything that could happen on a space mission—anything that could go wrong. In training things keep breaking, problems have to be solved .. . I started my formal NASA training in 1990. During that period I spent about half of the time in training, the other half I spent performing other duties. I was in training for three years before my first mission, which isn't that long of a wait. Some astronauts have waited ten, even sixteen years before they finally go into space!"

Ochoa traveled to the Johnson Space Center in Houston, Texas, for her training. During this time she married a man named Coe Fulmer Miles, who accompanied Ochoa to Texas. Astronaut trainees spend one or two years in Texas at the Johnson Space

This is an aerial view of the Johnson Space Center in Houston, Texas. This is where Ellen Ochoa received much of her astronaut training, beginning in 1990, in preparation for her first shuttle flight in 1993. Training involved intense study, difficult physical tests, exhausting survival training, and thrilling jet piloting.

Center learning the ropes. There they receive training in scuba diving (which simulates the weightlessness of space), sea and land survival techniques, jet piloting, and the use of space suits. Trainees also take many classes, studying a wide range of subjects related to space flight and exploration, including math, geology, meteorology, navigation, orbital dynamics, astronomy, and physics. They read manuals and take computer-based training on orbiter systems ranging from propulsion (the firing of rockets to create forward movement) to life support (the supply and delivery of oxygen, water, and food).

To prepare astronauts for the disorienting sense of weightlessness they will experience in space, they are given a ride in a modified KC-135 jet air-craft. The plane soars through the sky in a steep arc. As it reaches its highest point of altitude, it noses down and begins a steep but controlled descent. For twenty to thirty seconds, as the plane is cresting at its highest altitude, a momentary sense of weightlessness is created. The plane will make thirty to forty of these "parabolas" in a single flight. The KC-135 is nicknamed "the vomit comet" for the effect it has on many trainees'

stomachs. Astronauts must learn to work in this environment despite the nausea.

A gentler way to simulate weightlessness is found in the Weightless Environment Training Facility (WETF). This is a large tank that is filled with water and contains the same kind of equipment that astronauts will use and operate in space. Wearing special scuba suits, the trainees enter the tank and get a good feel for what it will be like to work in a microgravity environment (conditions in which gravity is small or reduced). The equipment in the tank is not functional, but the simulation helps the trainees get used to the sensation of moving around and performing manual tasks in weightless conditions.

Astronaut trainees also use Shuttle Mission Simulators (SMS)—machines that closely replicate many of the space shuttle's systems and functions, allowing astronauts to practice a wide range of normal and emergency mission situations. The SMS provides trainees with a taste of what launch feels like with its powerful vibrations and heavy weight of G-forces (gravitational forces). During a shuttle takeoff, astronauts are exposed to about 3.2 Gs, or

Flight and survival training were crucial elements in Ellen Ochoa's preparations for space flight. At top, Ochoa is seen in the rear cockpit of a T-38A jet at Ellington Field near the Johnson Space Center in 1990. At bottom, wearing a helmet and flight suit, Ochoa performs a water survival exercise in a pool.

3.2 times the force of gravity experienced on Earth. The often rocky ride of reentry into Earth's atmosphere can be simulated as well in the SMS. Trainees spend hundreds of hours in the SMS familiarizing themselves with all aspects of the space shuttle's operations and the tasks associated with the major phases of the flight—prelaunch, takeoff, ascent, orbit, and entry and landing.

The instructors want to make sure that each astronaut has a thorough understanding of every shuttle operation and procedure and enough knowledge to be able to react effectively to anything that may go wrong in space. An astronaut should never be surprised by a situation but should instead respond with a well-rehearsed series of actions. The SMS allows trainees to gain this crucial knowledge and hands-on experience. By the time they get to space for the first time, their tasks should feel routine, even if nothing has prepared them for the stunning view!

Discovery

Most astronaut trainees wait a long time before being assigned to their first space flight. Ellen

Flight simulators help astronauts experience close approximations of takeoff, reentry, and landing, as well as possible emergency situations that require problem solving. In this picture, Ellen Ochoa and fellow astronaut Michael Bloomfield are taking part in a simulator exercise at the Johnson Space Center.

Ochoa, however, was chosen to go on a mission after only three years of training. She was assigned to the STS–56 mission, aboard the space shuttle *Discovery*, scheduled for April 1993. On this mission, Ochoa would serve as mission specialist and perform a series of experiments, including a study of the effects of solar activity on Earth.

MAE JEMISON, THE FIRST AFRICAN AMERICAN WOMAN IN SPACE

Mae Jemison was born in Decatur, Alabama, on October 17, 1956, but grew up in Chicago, Illinois. She was an excellent student and especially skilled in science. Jemison, a graduate of Stanford University, was a medical doctor before she became an astronaut. From 1983 to 1985, she worked as a Peace Corps medical officer. In 1985, after her time in the Peace Corps, she worked as a general practitioner in Los Angeles.

Jemison made history on September 12, 1992, when she boarded the space shuttle *Endeavor* for the STS-47 Spacelab J mission and became the first African American woman to journey to space. She was a science mission specialist on this flight, which was a joint mission between the United States and Japan. Jemison's main job was to conduct several scientific experiments, including a study of the behavior of bone cells in space. Bone cells tend to break down more quickly in microgravity, a process that may yield clues to slowing bone loss in the elderly back on Earth.

Although she had taken part in only one space mission, Jemison resigned from NASA in 1993. She turned her attention to helping those less fortunate than herself by starting The Earth We Share (TEWS), an organization that sponsors a space camp for teens and encourages science literacy for all students. At the space camp, students ranging in age from twelve to sixteen are provided with instruction in the math and science skills they will need in order to become astronauts.

As a tribute to her historic achievements and her commitment to the education of America's youth, the Mae C. Jemison Academy, an alternative public school in Detroit, Michigan, was opened in 1992. Jemison felt extremely honored to have a public school named in her honor.

Ochoa would be boarding the space shuttle *Discovery* with four other astronauts—all men. Ellen was one of two astronauts in the group who had never been in space before. The unfamiliar and stressful conditions of actual—rather than simulated—space travel would no doubt provide a challenge for the two rookies, but there was no turning

Dressed in the training versions of the space suits worn by astronauts during takeoff and reentry, Ellen Ochoa and fellow astronaut Joseph Tanner prepare for a training session on emergency egress procedures. An emergency egress is the exiting from a spacecraft during an unexpected accident.

back now. Her numerous attempts over several years to gain entry into NASA, the long, exhausting hours of examinations and training, and the many years of education were all leading to this very moment. Ochoa had earned an opportunity that many people can only dream of. Ochoa was, as always, prepared, confident, and curious. According to *Contemporary Heroes and Heroines, Book IV*, Ochoa said, "What everyone in the astronaut corps shares in common is not gender or ethnic background, but motivation, perseverance, and desire—the desire to participate in a voyage of discovery."

CHAPTER 4

UP IN SPACE

By early 1993, Ellen Ochoa had paid her dues at NASA and was awaiting the chance of a lifetime. She was fully trained, used to the feeling of weightlessness, prepared for unexpected emergencies, and ready to make her first trip into space. It would also be the very first space flight for a Hispanic woman. At the age of thirty-four, Ellen Ochoa was making history.

STS-56

The crew of the space shuttle *Discovery* was due to take off into space on April 6, 1993. As they prepared for takeoff, however, there were indications of a problem with some of the machinery on the space shuttle. The shuttle was carefully checked out, but nothing was found to be wrong. Two days later, on April 8, Ellen Ochoa and the rest of the *Discovery* crew blasted off into space.

The nine-day STS-56 mission involved a study of the Sun and the ozone layer. As mission specialist, Ochoa was responsible for conducting the scientific studies that would try to measure the effects of the Sun's energy on Earth's atmosphere, its environment, and the functioning of satellites. As Ochoa explained to Anne Hart of GraduatingEngineer.com:

> *On my first flight, we studied ozone depletion of the Earth's atmosphere. We measured a wide variety of chemicals in the air. Measuring the concentration at different altitudes and the amount of energy coming from the sun were a way to understand important atmospheric chemical reactions. We took measurements during the entire mission which are put into a precise database and later used to correct and recalibrate instruments and data on orbiting satellites.*

During this mission the crew also was responsible for sending off and then capturing a 2,800-pound (1,270-kilogram) satellite called *Spartan*, which was designed to study the Sun's corona—the atmosphere at the Sun's edge that often looks like a circle of light. Ochoa used the Remote Manipulator System (RMS)—a large robotic arm—to maneuver the satellite into and out of the shuttle's cargo bay. Handling large, heavy objects with the robotic arm is very difficult and requires many hours of training. Typically, Ochoa rose to the challenge. As she explained in an interview with Scholastic.com:

I have worked the robot arm on all three of my space missions, and I really love it. It's challenging to do, but lots of fun. On my last mission to the space station, I worked with the help of cameras and monitors because we were docked in a way

At 1 AM on April 8, 1993, the space shuttle *Discovery* takes off from the Kennedy Space Center in Florida, carrying a crew of five, including Ellen Ochoa. Mission STS-56, as this space flight was called, was designed to study the effects on the ozone layer of the Sun's energy output and the chemicals of Earth's middle atmosphere.

that prevented me from seeing the robot arm. This made things more difficult, but then again, everything I've done on actual missions in space has always been easier than when I first tried it during training.

The Crew

The *Discovery* crew consisted of five astronauts, including Ochoa. She was joined by Kenneth D. Cameron, commander; Stephen S. Oswald, pilot; C. Michael Foale, mission specialist; and Kenneth D. Cockrell, mission specialist. Like Ochoa, each of these men had successfully completed NASA's long application and training process. They were each knowledgeable in their chosen field. Together, they formed a strong team.

Before joining NASA in 1984, Kenneth Cameron had been a member of the U.S. Marine Corps for many years. During his first space mission in 1991, he served as the shuttle pilot, an awesome responsibility for a rookie astronaut and one that requires a cool head and nerves of steel. He had no shortage of piloting experience. In fact, over the course of his lifetime, he has logged

This is a portrait of the five crew members of STS-56 taken shortly before their space flight. Top row, left to right: mission specialist C. Michael Foale, Commander Kenneth D. Cameron, and mission specialist Ellen Ochoa. Bottom row, left to right: mission specialist Kenneth D. Cockrell and pilot Stephen S. Oswald.

more than 4,000 hours of flying time in many different kinds of aircraft.

Stephen Oswald graduated from the U.S. Naval Academy in 1973. Just one year later he became a naval aviator—a person who flies planes for the U.S. Navy. The STS-56 mission was his second space flight with NASA. In total he has been on three NASA missions.

STS-56 was C. Michael Foale's second trip to space, but not his last. He has participated in five space missions and has performed three space walks.

Kenneth Cockrell had never been on a mission before STS-56. Like Ochoa, he had only recently completed astronaut training. Today, he is a veteran of five space flights and has logged more than 1,500 hours in space.

While up in space, the crew had the unique opportunity to talk to kids in schools throughout the United States. With the help of the Shuttle Amateur Radio Experiment II (SAREX II), they also made radio contact with Russia's *Mir* Space Station. This was the first contact ever made between a shuttle and the *Mir* Space Station using amateur radio equipment.

What Was It Like Up in Space?

The atmosphere up in space is much different than the atmosphere on Earth. For this reason, being in space takes some getting used to. The first thing one would notice in space is that there is no gravity. Gravity is the unseen force that pulls objects toward

STS 56 pilot Stephen S. Oswald sits at the pilot's station in the shuttle's forward flight deck and communicates with amateur radio operators, including schoolchildren, on Earth using equipment designed for the Shuttle Amateur Radio Experiment II (SAREX II). The experiment was meant to encourage public participation in the space program.

Ellen Ochoa handles a 35-mm camera on the *Discovery's* rear flight deck during STS-56.

the ground. When we walk, gravity keeps us from floating in the air; it pulls us toward Earth. Being in the zero gravity of space means that people and things are seemingly weightless; they float freely. Imagine how many times a day you place things down on a table or counter, knowing that they will stay exactly where you put them. In space, you can not just put something down and count on finding it there again later. It will float away!

Astronauts have to change their behavior to accommodate the lack of gravity in space. Ochoa compared the sensation of weightlessness to swimming or scuba diving because she had a certain freedom of movement that she had never felt on dry land. This is why NASA uses scuba diving and water tanks as astronaut training tools. It is the closest thing to the feeling of weightlessness that exists on Earth.

Sleeping on the space shuttle also took some getting used to. Because there were not enough beds to go around and someone had to be awake at all times, Ochoa and the other shuttle astronauts slept in two shifts. One group would stay up while the others slept, and then they would switch. They did not sleep in regular beds. Instead, they rested in sleeping bags equipped with restraints to prevent the astronauts from floating away. Bill Shepard, the commander of the first International Space Station crew, explained what sleeping in space was like to *National Geographic*: "Sleeping in space is very relaxing. You're not weighed down by gravity, so you don't feel anything pressing on your skin."

There is no fresh food on the space shuttle. Astronauts are instead given freeze-dried meals to eat. This is food that is preserved by being frozen very quickly and then dried by a high-powered vacuum. These food packets are easy to store and are compact, and they require no refrigeration. To eat this food, the astronauts add hot water to restore the moisture and make it warm. Foods that crumble, such as cookies and cakes, cannot be brought along in the space shuttle. In zero gravity, crumbs would not fall to the shuttle floor where they could then be swept up and thrown away. In space, crumbs would float throughout the space shuttle, possibly getting into and damaging sensitive machinery and instruments. There are no refrigerators on space shuttles, so astronauts never get cold food or drinks. Despite these limitations, astronauts are provided with over seventy kinds of food and twenty kinds of drink powders to which water is added. Astronauts are careful to store all trash and bring it back to Earth. They are not allowed to release it into space or let it float around the space shuttle.

Zero gravity also makes going to the bathroom a real challenge. In fact, astronauts use bathrooms specially designed to solve the gravity problem. As Ochoa explained to Scholastic.com:

There is a special bathroom area on board that looks almost like the same toilet you would see at home or at school. The difference is that instead of gravity, there is an air-flow system to move the waste along. There are two separate systems—one for the solid waste and one for the urine. The waste gets stored in on-board tanks, which are cleaned out when the shuttle returns to Earth. The bathrooms on the shuttle aren't as convenient as the ones on Earth, but you get used to it.

Space toilets are not the only unusual element in the shuttle bathroom. There are also no showers or baths. Instead, astronauts keep clean by giving themselves sponge baths. They can brush their teeth in the normal way, though they have to be careful not to drip any toothpaste—it would just float away!

While orbiting overhead in the space shuttle, there are many ways to stay in touch with people on Earth—including radios and closed-circuit and satellite television. Ochoa communicated with her husband by e-mail while in space. Generally, however, if a space mission lasts more than ten days, astronauts can use a videophone to talk to loved ones. A videophone allows the people speaking on either end to see each other as well as hear each other's voices.

This is a photograph of the space shuttle *Discovery*'s cargo bay, with its doors open and Earth visible below. The bay holds the Atmospheric Laboratory for Applications and Science (ATLAS-2), in which the mission's studies of the ozone layer were conducted.

While up in space, astronauts lose muscle mass quickly, an unfortunate effect of weightlessness. On Earth, gravity presses against one's body, making muscles have to work to withstand the pressure. They bulk up as a result. In zero gravity, muscles encounter no resistance, so they begin to waste away. Astronauts combat this by exercising frequently. Treadmills, rowing machines, and stationary bikes are installed in the space shuttle to help the astronauts prevent excessive muscle loss.

In their free time, astronauts have been known to read books, watch movies, and take pictures of Earth from space. Free time, however, is not something astronauts have in abundance. Between performing many complex experiments, tending to the shuttle, checking in with mission control, eating, sleeping, and exercising, there is not much time left for playing around. Astronauts try to have fun while they are on the space shuttle. Much of their pleasure comes from the awe-inspiring views outside of their windows.

The most fascinating moments of Ochoa's first space mission were not the scientific studies she

A TRIBUTE

During Ochoa's second space shuttle mission in November 1994, she carried with her the class ring of a young woman named Stacey Lynn Balascio. Stacey was a student at San Diego State University studying aerospace engineering when she was hit by a car and killed just four days before graduating from college on May 24, 1994. Both Balascio and Ochoa had grown up in La Mesa, California, and had attended Grossmont High School. They were both interested in engineering and excelled in their schoolwork. Ochoa took Balascio's class ring into space with her as a tribute to this young woman whose life—as full of promise as Ochoa's—was cut short. When she landed back on Earth, Ochoa presented the ring to Stacey's parents.

performed or the data she helped to collect. For her, the greatest interest lay in the simple beauty of space. From their unique vantage point, astronauts can clearly see the beautiful blues and greens of Earth below. It is a rare and majestic sight that Ochoa would see several more times in her life.

Ellen Ochoa was dazzled by the sheer beauty of space and Earth below during her first shuttle mission. She is seen here with a 70-mm camera, photographing an ocean scene from the shuttle's overhead window.

Return to Space

The space shuttle *Discovery* landed back on Earth on April 17, 1993, at 7:37 AM. Ochoa had completed her first assignment as a mission specialist, and it was a huge success. Her dream of going into space had officially been fulfilled. Ochoa's years of diligent study, hard work, and tireless determination had paid off. Yet she was by no means finished with her career as an astronaut. There was more work to be done and, most important to Ochoa, much more to be learned.

On November, 3, 1994, Ochoa returned to space. This time she was traveling on board the space shuttle *Atlantis* on mission STS-66. The mission's objective was to continue NASA's earlier studies on the Sun and its effect on Earth's atmosphere. This time, she was not only a mission specialist, but she also was given the title of payload commander. As payload commander, Ochoa was in charge of the mission's scientific studies. Their success rested on her shoulders. Once again she used the RMS, the robotic arm, to retrieve a satellite that

On April 8, 2002, Ellen Ochoa made her fourth shuttle flight aboard *Atlantis*. The crew was sent to deliver supplies to the crew of the International Space Station. In this picture, Ochoa *(center)*, Michael Bloomfield *(far right)*, and Rex Walheim *(left)* are secured to the shuttle's seats moments before launch.

had been sent into orbit to perform atmospheric studies. This space flight was the third shuttle mission to conduct atmospheric studies. This time around, the focus was on the large hole in the ozone layer that was opening up over Antarctica. The flight lasted eleven days and returned safely. During the flight, Ochoa entertained herself and her fellow astronauts by playing the flute.

Ochoa and the International Space Station

Ochoa's third space flight was on the STS-96 mission from May 27 to June 6, 1999. This flight also lasted ten days. In that time, the crew members delivered four tons of supplies to the International Space Station (ISS) during the first docking ever between a space shuttle and the ISS. These supplies, some of them guided to the ISS by Ochoa and the shuttle's robotic arm during an eight-hour space walk, would allow the soon-to-arrive first crew of the space station to begin their important scientific research.

The ISS is a large laboratory that orbits Earth and is a temporary home and office to visiting astronaut-scientists who conduct research in space. Sixteen nations, including the United States, Russia, Japan, Canada, and Brazil, and the European Space Agency came together to fund, build, and staff the station. Construction of the ISS began in 1998 and has continued through 2004. It is being built in stages, with the help of space walks and robots, as more than forty space

flights over several years have ferried materials from Earth to the growing space station. If completed as planned, it will weigh more than 1 million pounds (453,592 kilograms) and include six laboratories. Inside, it will have about the same volume as the cabin of a 747 jumbo jet. The exterior's surface area will be larger than a football field.

The reason the International Space Station was built is because the weightlessness that occurs in space—sometimes referred to as microgravity—makes for a unique environment in which scientific studies can be performed free of the distorting effects of gravity. Areas of research such as fluid flow, the behavior of fire, and growth of cells and crystals are especially suited to microgravity and have implications for fire fighting, agriculture, and cancer treatment. The effect of microgravity on the

During Ellen Ochoa's third shuttle mission, STS-96, on board the *Discovery*, she would supervise an enormous delivery of supplies from the shuttle to the International Space Station. The shuttle carried tons of supplies up into space for the men aboard the ISS. The shuttle's robotic arm, operated by Ochoa, hauled many of the supplies from the shuttle to the ISS.

structure and function of the brain, nerves, muscles, bones, and immune system is another valuable avenue of research and has implications here on Earth for understanding the aging process and improving health care.

The ISS provides a permanent platform for long-range experiments. Before the International Space Station, astronauts had only a short time to conduct experiments in space. When it was time to return to Earth, it was time to end the experiment. Now, studies conducted on the space station can be ongoing and monitored by the various crews assigned to the ISS for limited periods and scientists here on Earth.

The space station also has the ability to take daily high-resolution pictures of Earth from space, allowing scientists to observe any important changes in Earth's atmosphere. Changes in climate, pollution levels, and tree cover in rain forests, for example, can all be measured by the crystal clear and highly detailed photographs taken from the ISS.

It is costing many countries millions of dollars to build and maintain the International Space Station.

But many people believe that the money is well worth it because the discoveries that result from the experiments performed on the International Space Station may greatly improve the quality of life on Earth.

From April 8 to April 19, 2002, Ochoa traveled back to the International Space Station. This eleven-day mission, called STS-110, was on the *Atlantis*, a space shuttle that Ochoa was familiar with from her second mission. It was the thirteenth time a shuttle docked with the ISS. For the first time ever, the shuttle's robotic arm was used to move crew members during a space walk around the ISS. The arm was also used to install equipment on the space station.

After all of this high-altitude excitement, one might think that Ellen Ochoa is ready to take it easy for a while. After all, since 1990, she has dedicated most of her time to NASA, training, traveling into space, and performing important scientific research. Predictably, however, Ochoa is not interested in slowing down anytime soon. In fact, she currently serves as the deputy director of flight crew operations at Johnson Space Center

STS-110, Ellen Ochoa's fourth shuttle mission, featured the delivery of equipment to the International Space Station. In this picture, the shuttle's robotic arm, operated by Ochoa, hauls a truss segment, called S Zero (S0), to the ISS. The S Zero is a 43-foot-long (13-m) structure weighing 27,000 pounds (12,247 kg). It forms the center of what will eventually be a nine-truss, girderlike structure that will extend the length of a football field.

and hopes to return to space before too long. Ellen Ochoa is not one to rest on her laurels. Her curiosity, energy, and intelligence will not let her slow down!

CONCLUSION

A NEW BEGINNING

Ellen Ochoa had led a full life even before being selected for NASA's shuttle program. Graduating valedictorian of her high school and college classes is an amazing achievement. Graduating with honors from a top university is another incredible feat. Even before getting recognition as the first Hispanic woman to travel to space, she had invented optical systems for which she was given patents by the United States government. Her outstanding research for Sandia National Laboratories and NASA's Ames Research Center also brought her recognition and acclaim.

Now, after her inspiring triumphs in space and on the ground with NASA, Ochoa continues to lead a

full life. She has a husband and two children. Before the birth of her second child, Ochoa was asked in an interview with Scholastic.com how she is able to be both an astronaut and a mother, Ochoa had this to say:

> *I think it's hard being anything and a mother. Both are full-time jobs, and you have to work very hard at both to do a good job. Personally, I find both jobs wonderful. It is hard to be separated from my husband and son when I go on a mission, and I miss them a great deal. But lots of people have to be away from their families because of their jobs. Right now my son is only 18 months old, so the last time I went into space, he didn't really know what was going on. I think it will be much harder the next time since he will understand more.*

Wilson, Ellen's first son, was too young to understand why his mother was gone for a period of time. It was hard for them to be separated from each other. Before a mission, the astronauts are quarantined, or put into isolation, for one week so they will be less likely to get sick during a mission. Considering the time that Ochoa had to

Ellen Ochoa is reunited with her son, Wilson Miles-Ochoa, on June 6, 1999, following her return to the Kennedy Space Center in Florida from shuttle mission STS-96 aboard the *Discovery*. Ochoa says that being separated during space flights is hard on mother and child alike.

be quarantined, she was away from her family for three weeks.

In an interview with CNN conducted before the birth of her second son, Ochoa described one way she had discovered to remain close to her son while up in space. Before one of her missions, she made a special tape for Wilson to watch when he missed his mom: "It's of me doing things with him that my husband can show him every night while I'm gone. And that way he'll get a chance to see me every day even though I won't be there in person."

In addition to spending as much free time as possible with her husband and children, Ochoa also has many hobbies that keep her busy, such as bicycling, volleyball, and playing the flute. Ochoa's real passion is talking to schoolchildren and sharing the wisdom her mother passed on to her. She has given numerous talks to students, encouraging them to work hard in school and set high goals for themselves. After all, she is real-life proof that hard work can make even the most lofty dreams come true.

Ochoa has spoken to thousands of students about her adventures both in space and on Earth. As she explained during an interview with Lydia Martin of

Ellen Ochoa returned from her fourth shuttle mission on April 19, 2002, after an eleven-day trip in space. After landing at the Kennedy Space Center, she flew to Houston to take part in a crew return ceremony at the Johnson Space Center. She is seen here addressing the assembled crowd of well-wishers.

the Knight-Ridder/Tribune News Service, "I do as much speaking as I'm allowed to do. I tell students that the opportunities I had were a result of having a very good educational background. Education is what allows you to stand out." Ochoa wants to influence the way children think about possible careers. She feels that if they plan from an early age, they will be better prepared to achieve their goals. On the

Stanford University Web site, Ochoa is quoted as saying, "I've probably given 150 talks over the past few years. I never thought about this aspect of the job when I was applying, but it's extremely rewarding. I'm not trying to make every kid an astronaut, but I want kids to think about a career and the preparation they'll need."

Ochoa also travels to speak with kids about NASA in particular. NASA has always been interested in educating the public about what it does and how its work impacts our society in a positive way. Ochoa told Anne Hart of GraduatingEngineer.com:

> *We take a trip about once a month as part of our job. Students are excited to meet someone who has been to outer space. Everyone wants to know more about space careers for engineers and scientists. They all ask me to detail how it feels to live in space. They want me to tell them what they'll be doing in space in the future . . . The high school and university students most frequently ask me what purpose I have being in space. They ask me to detail what I do in my work and what I plan to do in the future.*

As a prominent member of the Hispanic community, Ochoa likes to reach out to Hispanic students in particular, to inspire them to do great things. In 2001, Ellen reached out to her community to encourage some of its younger members to become teachers. According to *La Prensa San Diego*, she said, "A hallmark of the Latino community is to help one another. If students are interested in a way to give back and help their communities, becoming a teacher is probably one of the very best ways of doing that."

During her lifetime, Ochoa has received many awards for her work. NASA alone has awarded her with the Exceptional Service Medal in 1997; the Outstanding Leadership Medal in 1995; Space Flight Medals in 1993, 1994, 1999, and 2002; and two Space Act Tech Brief Awards in 1992. The awards from NASA were for her many contributions and dedication to the space program.

She has also been offered many honors by other organizations. She was given the Women in Aerospace Outstanding Achievement Award, the Hispanic Engineer Albert Baez Award for Outstanding

Ellen Ochoa is seen here with fellow female astronauts during a July 19, 1999, conference at the Kennedy Space Center on women in the space industry. From left to right are Ochoa, Joan Higginbotham, Yvonne Cagle, and Sally Ride, the first American woman in space.

Technical Contribution to Humanity, the Hispanic Heritage Leadership Award, and the San Diego State University Alumna of the Year Award.

Most recently, Ochoa was honored by the U.S. State Department. On March 10, 2003, Ellen became the first honoree for the 2003 Women's History Month. Each year, women whose efforts have contributed to the United States's rich and diverse history are honored in the month of March, Women's History Month.

As a young girl, Ellen Ochoa never imagined that she would one day join NASA and travel into space to perform research and scientific study. All she knew was what her mother had always told her: Get a good education and you can be whatever you want to be. Ochoa quickly developed a passion for learning and a desire to always discover new things. Never one to back down from a challenge, she constantly pushed herself to explore new directions and acquire as much knowledge as possible. From high school to college to graduate school, Ochoa always demonstrated a maturity, dedication, determination, and intelligence that were beyond her years. Even though she pushed herself hard, she always made time for fun. She became an accomplished classical flutist and even found the time to learn how to fly planes. She is still an active member of NASA's astronaut program and may go up into space again soon.

During her past four shuttle missions, Ochoa has logged more than 700 hours in space and performed numerous space walks. As a mission specialist, she learned how to use the shuttle's robotic arm to move equipment and people around in space. She also performed research for NASA, both up in orbit and on land. Her work is as varied as can be, thanks partly to the fact that her many interests and talents have enabled her to be good at many things. It seems certain that Ellen Ochoa would be good at almost anything she tried.

Though Ochoa is a woman in a field dominated by men, she has not been intimidated. And though there had never been a Hispanic female astronaut before her, she did not let that influence her decision to become one. Instead, she forged ahead and became a pioneer in her field.

Ellen Ochoa sits aboard the International Space Station and gazes down on Earth during her fourth shuttle mission, STS-110, on April 16, 2002. Now deputy director of flight crew operations at NASA, Ochoa hopes to be given another chance to return to space. Determined and spirited as ever, Ochoa continues to reach for the stars.

Ellen Ochoa's life is an inspiration to us all, regardless of race, gender, or ethnicity. From her story, we learn that hard work does pay off and that getting a good education can take you wherever you want to go, even as far as outer space. Ellen Ochoa reached for the stars and blasted off into greatness.

GLOSSARY

alumni People who have graduated from a certain school or university.

ascent The act of going upward; on incline.

atmosphere The mass of air surrounding Earth.

dissertation A formal paper that explores a topic in great detail, usually written by a person seeking an advanced academic degree.

engineering The application of scientific and mathematical principles to the design, manufacture, and operation of machines or systems.

gravity The natural force that draws people and objects to Earth's surface.

heritage Attributes or traditions that are passed down from one generation of a group to the succeeding generations.

minority A member of an ethnic, religious, or other group that is distinct from and smaller than the society's largest and most powerful group.

orbit The path that a celestial body or artificial satellite takes around another body.

patent An official document that grants an inventor the sole right to use his or her invention.

physics The science of matter and energy and how the two interact.

psychological Having to do with the mind or emotions.

quarantine To be placed in enforced isolation in order to prevent the spread of disease.

satellite An object that is launched into space to orbit Earth or another celestial body, like the Moon or planets.

scholar A person who is knowledgeable in a certain academic field.

solar Having to do with the Sun.

strenuous Something that is difficult or requires the expense of great energy.

valedictorian A student who has earned the highest grades of his or her graduating class.

videophone A telephone that allows its users to
see and hear one another during a conversation.
weightlessness Having little gravitational pull;
seeming to have no weight.

FOR MORE INFORMATION

American Astronautical Society
6352 Rolling Mill Place, Suite 102
Springfield, VA 22152-2354
(703) 866-0020
Web site: http://www.astronautical.org

Goddard Space Flight Center
Code 130, Office of Public Affairs
Greenbelt, MD 20771
(301) 286-8955
Web site: http://www.gsfc.nasa.gov

Jet Propulsion Laboratory
Public Services Office

Mail Stop 186-113
4800 Oak Grove Drive
Pasadena, CA 91109
(818) 354-9314
Web site: http://www.jpl.nasa.gov

Johnson Space Center
Visitors Center
1601 NASA Road 1
Houston, TX 77058
(281) 244-2100
Web site: http://www.jsc.nasa.gov

Kennedy Space Center Visitor Complex
Mail Code: DNPS
Kennedy Space Center, FL 32899
(321) 449-4444
Web site: http://www.kennedyspacecenter.com

NASA Headquarters
Information Center
Washington, DC 20546-0001
(202) 358 0000
Web site: http://www.nasa.gov

Space Policy Institute
1957 E Street NW, Suite 403
Washington, DC 20052
(202) 994-7292
Web site: http://www.gwu.edu/~spi/

United States Strategic Command
Public Affairs Office
901 Sac Boulevard, Suite 1A1
Offutt Air Force Base, NE 68113-6020
(402) 294-4130
Web site: http://www.spacecom.mil

U.S. Space Camp
P.O. Box 070015
Huntsville, AL 35807-7015
(800) 533-7281
(256) 721-7150
Web site: http://www.spacecamp.com/home.asp

Web Sites

Due to the changing nature of Internet links, the Rosen Publishing Group, Inc., has developed an online list of Web sites related to the subject of this book. This site is updated regularly. Please use this link to access the list:

http://www.rosenlinks.com/lasb/eoch

FOR FURTHER READING

Atkins, Jeannine. *Wings and Rockets: The Story of Women in Air and Space.* New York: Farrar, Straus & Giroux, 2003.

Corrigan, Grace George. *A Journal for Christa: Christa McAuliffe, Teacher in Space.* New York: Bison Books Corporation, 2000.

Freni, Pamela S. *Space for Women: A History of Women with the Right Stuff.* Santa Ana, CA: Seven Locks Press, 2002.

Hopping, Lorraine Jean. *Sally Ride: Space Pioneer.* New York: McGraw Hill, 2000.

Lassieur, Allison. *The Space Shuttle.* New York: Children's Press, 2000.

Marvis, Barbara J. *Contemporary American Success Stories: Famous People of Hispanic Heritage: Geraldo Rivera, Melissa Gonzalez, Federico Pena, Ellen Ochoa. Bear, DE: Mitchell* Lane Publishers, Inc., 1995.

Romero, Maritza. *Ellen Ochoa: The First Hispanic Woman Astronaut*. New York: The Rosen Publishing Group, Inc., 1998.

Sinott, Susan. *Extraordinary Hispanic Americans*. Danbury, CT: Children's Press, 1995.

St. John, Jetty. *Hispanic Scientists*. Mankato, MN: Capstone Press, 1996.

Taylor, Robert. *The Space Shuttle*. San Diego: Lucent Books, 2001.

Walker, Pam. *Ellen Ochoa*. New York: Children's Press, 2001.

BIBLIOGRAPHY

"Celebrate Hispanic Heritage, Meet Famous Latinos: Ellen Ochoa." Scholastic. com. 1999. Retrieved March 2003 (http://teacher.scholastic.com/ activities/hispanic/ochoatscript.htm).

"Dr. Ellen Ochoa: Education . . . The Stepping Stone to the Stars." La Prensa San Diego. December 7, 2001. Retrieved March 2003 (http://www.laprensa-sandiego.org/archive/ december07/OCHOA.HTM).

"Ellen Ochoa, Ph.D. '85, MS '81 Electrical Engineering: A Higher Education." Stanford University School of Engineering. 2000. Retrieved March 2003 (http://www.soe.stanford.edu/ AR97-98/ochoa.html).

Finton, Nancy. *"Living It Up in Space."* National Geographic.com. October 2001. Retrieved March 2003 (http://magma.nationalgeographic.com/ngexplorer/0110/articles/iss_0110.html).

Hart, Anne. *"Without Limits."* GraduatingEngineer.com. 1999. Retrieved March 2003 (http://www.graduatingengineer.com/articles/minority/11-12-99.html).

"HSF-STS=110 Crew Interviews, Preflight Interview: Ellen Ochoa." NASA. April 2002. Retrieved March 2003 (http://spaceflight.nasa.gov/shuttle/archives/sts-110/crew/intochoa.html).

Jenkins, Dennis R. *Space Shuttle: The History of the National Space Transportation System: The First 100 Missions.* North Branch, MN: Specialty Press and Publishers Wholesalers, Inc., 2001.

Marvis, Barbara J. *Contemporary American Success Stories: Famous People of Hispanic Heritage: Geraldo Rivera, Melissa Gonzalez, Federico Pena, Ellen Ochoa.* Bear, DE: Mitchell Lane Publishers, Inc., 1995.

"NASA Biographical Data: Ellen Ochoa." NASA. January 2003. Retrieved March 2003 (http://www.jsc.nasa.gov/Bios/htmlbios/ochoa.html).

O'Brien, Miles. *"Getting to Know the Crew of STS-96."* CNN.com. May 1999. Retrieved March 2003 (http://www.cnn.com/TECH/space/9905/24/downlinks/#2).

Reichardt, Tony, ed. *Space Shuttle: The First 20 Years: The Astronauts' Experiences in Their Own Words.* New York: DK Publishing, 2002.

"STS-56 Press Kit." NASA. 2000. Retrieved March 2003 (http://science.ksc.nasa.gov/shuttle/missions/sts-56/sts-56-press-kit.txt).

Woodmansee, Laura S. *Women Astronauts.* Toronto, Ontario: Apogee Books, 2002.

INDEX

ELLEN OCHOA

About the Author

Joy Paige is a writer and editor living in New York City. She enjoys arts and crafts, water sports, and stamp collecting.

Photo Credits

Cover, pp. 1, 4–5, 46, 49, 51, 54, 59, 61, 63, 68–69, 72, 76, 80–81, 85, 87, 95 courtesy of NASA; pp. 8, 43 © Bettmann/Corbis; pp. 15, 28, 31, 36, 45, 64, 74, 92, 53 © AP/Wide World Photos; p. 19 © Richard Cummins/Corbis; p. 20 courtesy of San Diego State University; p. 39 © Lee Snider/Corbis.

Designer: Les Kanturek; Editor: John Kemmerer